Original title:
The Quietest Companions

Copyright © 2025 Creative Arts Management OÜ
All rights reserved.

Author: Nora Sinclair
ISBN HARDBACK: 978-1-80581-735-2
ISBN PAPERBACK: 978-1-80581-262-3
ISBN EBOOK: 978-1-80581-735-2

Beneath the Surface

In the depths of cozy nooks,
Where socks and dust bunnies play,
Lurks a friend with quirky looks,
Whispering tales by the light of day.

Under tables, soft and round,
Crisps and crumbs do take their seat,
With giggles caught, and laughter found,
They dance to a rhythm, oh so sweet.

When I'm lost in my own affair,
They'll tickle me with a gentle sweep,
While I grimace, sometimes stare,
A silent giggle before I sleep.

In the corners, secrets gleam,
With each bob and weave, they sway,
Ambassadors of the snack-time dream,
Absurd companions in their own way.

Solitude's Embrace

In the corner, a cat takes a nap,
Dreaming of mice, without a care,
A toast to silence, we raise a cup,
To furry friends who don't talk—fair!

Softly Spoken Bonds

A sandwich on the table, such glee,
I share a laugh with my loaf of bread,
Whispers of crunch in the harmony,
As crumbs dance lightly, no words are said.

Murmurs of Solace

The clock ticks slow, a gentle beat,
With every chime, a giggle erupts,
The tick-tock banter, oh so sweet,
My timepiece friend, how it disrupts!

Gentle Guardians

Beneath my desk, the dust bunnies play,
Whirling and twirling, they host a ball,
Silent but bold, in their own way,
Who knew that silence could be so small?

Secret Symphony

In the corner, a sock plays tunes,
While the dust bunnies dance to the moons.
A spatula conducts with flair,
As the fridge hums songs beyond compare.

The cat joins in with a meow and a purr,
While the plants nod gently, they seem to concur.
Together they make quite the show,
With laughter echoing, always aglow.

Softly Spoken Bonds

Between cushions, whispers take flight,
As the remote control joins the delight.
A t-shirt chuckles at laundry's plight,
While the closet giggles through the night.

Old shoes gather tales of a journey's end,
Each scuff a memory, a trusty friend.
They cheer each other, no need to pretend,
In this silent circle, their love won't bend.

The Art of Listening

A spoon leans in for the latest chat,
While a sleepy clock has a sly little spat.
The kettle spills secrets in steamy sighs,
As teabags gossip, oh how time flies!

The toaster pops, in delight it beams,
While butter and jam exchange quiet dreams.
In the kitchen, magic brews and teams,
As laughter simmers in gentle streams.

Unnoticed Embraces

Under the bed, a friendship blooms,
As lost toys uncover their secret rooms.
Dust particles waltz in a sunbeam's grace,
Cheering the shadows, a hidden embrace.

The old hat chuckles, a master of disguise,
While a lonely pen plots its own surprise.
In these still moments, joy quietly lies,
Embracing the stillness, under soft skies.

Under the Veil of Calm

In shadowy corners, a couch potato,
Gathering dust like a lazy tornado.
Socks on the floor, a little parade,
Witnessing battles of laundry crusade.

A hamster named Bob, he spins round and round,
His moody gaze says, 'I'm so profound!'
With eyes like saucers, he judges my snack,
As if he holds secrets I surely lack.

Muffled Heartbeats

In silence of night, the fridge gives a hum,
A serenade sweet, through the dark it will strum.
The cat on the sill gives a rebellious yawn,
While dreaming of fish in her fanciest dawn.

The toaster awaits for its glorious turn,
To pop up the bread like it's Sylvester's burn.
A squirrel on the roof laughs without a care,
Who knew my breakfast would end up in air?

Threads of Serenity

In the garden, the gnomes take care of the weeds,
Whispering secrets like they're the real steeds.
They've gathered together for a gnome concert,
Their instruments crafted from garden dirt.

The hedgehog chimes in with a prickly tone,
Says, 'We're the puns that you cannot disown!'
As petals fall down like confetti from trees,
My spirit is lifted with laughter's soft breeze.

Between Us, a Breath

A goldfish named Carl swims in loops of delight,
Dreaming of oceans, oh what a fun sight!
Each bubble he makes, like a burst of pure joy,
Echoing laughter, that's not just a ploy.

The clock on the wall ticks with such little grace,
Counting the moments in this cozy space.
While I munch on snacks with crumbs on my chin,
Laughing at moments where silliness wins.

Quietude in Unity

Two friends sit side by side,
In silence they confide.
One's eating chips so loud,
The other shouts, 'Be proud!'

They sip their tea with grace,
While making funny faces.
A burp escapes, oh dear!
Together they burst in cheer!

Breath of Serenity

A cat and dog in a race,
Chasing dust with happy grace.
The cat trips, she does a spin,
The pup just wags and grins.

In the sunbeam, they lie low,
Together, stealing the show.
A sneeze that shakes the ground,
In giggles, joy is found!

Hidden Threads of Trust

Two socks lost inside the wash,
With secrets, they make a posh.
One says, 'Let's start a band!'
The other rolls eyes, 'So bland!'

But with a twist and a swoosh,
They dance with a cloud of hush.
Swaying like they're on a spree,
In laughter, they both agree!

Silenced Laughter

A mouse and a cheese approach,
The cheese plays hard to broach.
The mouse, with a tiny squeak,
Makes a joke, oh what a peak!

With humor, they exchange winks,
In shadows, they chat and think.
Silent giggles, secret gleam,
In their laughter, wild dreams!

Awkward Emotions

In silence, we both sit and fidget,
Our laughs feel like they need a widget.
The awkward pause, a silly dance,
Each glance a game, a clumsy chance.

Your giggle breaks the frozen air,
Like pops of popcorn unaware.
We scribble notes on napkin dreams,
While coffee spills and chaos screams.

Veiled Bonds

Behind our masks, we play peek-a-boo,
Distant yet close, like morning dew.
A wink here, a nod there, quite absurd,
Who knew silence could speak every word?

Our secrets dance like fireflies at night,
Lit with giggles that feel just right.
While others chat about the mundane,
We share a smirk like a secret chain.

Tranquil Whispers

Your sofa is a ship of dreams,
Sailing down the lake of memes.
We whisper jokes in softest tones,
Floating through like gentle drones.

A bowl of chips, a shared delight,
Chasing crumbs with all our might.
We giggle low, it's such a thrill,
Our quiet bond, a cheeky spill.

Gentle Embrace

A hug that feels like fuzzy socks,
Wrapped tight around our silly knocks.
In stillness, laughter finds its home,
Two buddies lost in silly foam.

The world outside can spin and race,
But here, our smiles fill the space.
We dance to tunes only we hear,
Making merry, despite the cheer.

Words Left Unspoken

In a room filled with chatter, they plot their escape,
Two mice in the corner, a daring drape.
With a nibble and squeak, they aim for the cheese,
But the cat's watching close, with eyes full of tease.

Over teacups and biscuits, the humans all fret,
While our heroes steal crumbs, oh, what a set!
Whiskers twitching in glee, they dance under chairs,
For freedom's a feast if you've got the right cares.

As the clock ticks away and the night steals the show,
Those two little rascals put on quite the show.
With leaps and with twirls, they bring laughter and cheer,
In the shadows they dance, with nothing to fear.

Notes in the Silence

A fox in a hat wrote a song for the night,
With a chorus of crickets, all feeling quite bright.
In the hush of the woods, they tap dance on leaves,
While the fireflies flash, conjuring magic with ease.

An owl hoots along, but he's off key, you see,
Yet they embrace every note—such sweet harmony!
With a hiccup and hiccup, they laugh at the moon,
Tunes echo through shadows—oh, what a tune!

When shadows grow long and the fun starts to fade,
They gather their voices, not ready to trade.
For a giggle and wiggle, the night's still alive,
In the silence they flourish, oh how they thrive!

Company of Ghosts

In an old creaky mansion, the ghost do the jig,
Boo! Boo! they cry, while they each pop a big!
Spilling out laughter like fog on the stairs,
Every haunting is joyful; they hang out in pairs.

With a whoosh and a swirl, they throw a grand ball,
Cobbwebs for decoration, in the grand hall!
Tiptoeing softly, they dance with such flair,
Their laughter rings out, with a flip of their hair.

As midnight approaches, they shiver in glee,
Spinning tales of the past, just a ghostly spree.
In the company of shadows, they find their delight,
With stories and giggles, they light up the night.

Unfurling Silence

When the clock strikes the hour, and all seem asleep,
A piano plays softly, its secrets to keep.
With each gentle note, the dust starts to sway,
And cats on the windowsill join in the play.

In silence they gather, a splatter of sound,
As socks start to dance, twirling round and round.
With every soft shuffle, they break into song,
Where laughter erupts, heartbeats pulse strong.

The clock chimes the secrets, that linger so near,
But in this sweet stillness, there's nothing to fear.
For every lost whisper and chuckle profound,
Turns the quiet to magic, with joy all around.

Secrets of Stillness

In corners where dust bunnies play,
Lurks a whisper, what do they say?
They giggle and snicker without a sound,
In the stillness, mischief abound.

A cat watches closely, ears twitch with glee,
Pretending to nap, but what's really the key?
Her dreams are wild, I swear it's true,
Chasing threads of the softest blue.

The chair creaks softly when no one's near,
It's playing at ghosts,, spreading a cheer.
Hidden laughter in every chair leg's jig,
What a dance, but don't you dare gig!

Oh, the secrets that stillness can keep,
While the world rushes past, never to peep.
They roll on the floor, socks in a pile,
Loot from our laughter, if just for a while.

Shadows that Speak

Shadows gather, chatting away,
Bickering softly about the day.
One says, 'Did you see that shoe?'
'Oh, never mind, here's a story for you!'

A lamp flickers, winking in jest,
'Would you like to join our quiet fest?'
The curtains rustle, oh what a sight,
Plotting their pranks every night.

They swap little tales of lost keys and socks,
Of brave little mice who dance on the clocks.
And while they conspire in the dark,
We're blissfully unaware, blissfully spark!

When the night calls, and silence prevails,
There's mischief afoot in old tales.
And as we sleep, with dreams that dance,
Shadows prance on without a chance.

Unseen Allies

The fridge hums a tune, oh so sweet,
While the dust settles down to enjoy a treat.
They brag about crumbs and crumbs even more,
A gathering of snacks behind the kitchen door.

In the silence, a pencil rolls free,
It's got aspirations of finishing a spree.
A plot of paper whispered its name,
Unseen allies all in the game!

The sock peeks from the laundry pile high,
A secretive meeting under the sky.
It giggles at shirts with buttons undone,
In this world of quiet, there's never one.

Dust motes dance in their playful ballet,
As they greet each other, come what may.
They share silly stories as we snooze,
In this unseen kingdom, none can lose.

The Company of Silence

Whispers of nothing tickle my ear,
A brigade of silence, loud and clear.
They wiggle, they wiggle, with a skip and a hop,
A giggle parade that just doesn't stop!

Couches are fidgeting, itching to play,
While the curtains plot a getaway.
Invisible friends on this quiet night,
What fun is brewing just out of sight!

The clock ticks slowly with a knowing grin,
Counting the chuckles that bubble within.
An empty mug sings a song so bright,
'Fill me again for this whimsical flight!'

In the company of stillness, joy runs deep,
As in the dark, secrets leap.
So when you think no one's around,
Just listen closely; laughter's abound!

Gentle Presence

In a room so still and bright,
A dust bunny takes its flight,
It rolls with grace across the floor,
A silent friend, who needs no war.

With every whispered, tiny squeak,
It's the comfort that we seek,
A cushion soft, a shadow long,
In this quiet, we belong.

The cat pretends it's on a hunt,
But the dust winks, a soft affront,
Two pals share a sneaky glance,
In their own fuzzy, dust-filled dance.

When I stumble in a daze,
My secret friend is there to phase,
With laughter twinkling in its fluff,
Who needs more, when this is enough?

Calm Reflections

In the calm of morning light,
The spoon hums a tune so bright,
As I sip my coffee slow,
It giggles, putting on a show.

The blanket folds itself just right,
Wrapping me up in warmth and delight,
When I trip, it softly snickers,
A cozy hug, full of flickers.

A lazy sock on the floor sings,
Of lazy days and simple things,
With each little nudge it gives,
Who knew a sock could truly live?

In silence, they share a joke,
A tight-knit crew of every folk,
From mugs to spoons, they all reside,
In this calm, no need to hide.

The Unseen Embrace

When I feel a little blue,
My chair pretends it's hugging too,
A creaky laugh from an old wood beam,
Whispers softly, 'It's okay to dream.'

A forgotten book on the shelf,
Winks at me, 'Come read yourself!'
Its pages dance with tales to share,
Who knew stories had such flair?

Even dust on the window pane,
Becomes confetti in the rain,
As I twirl, it swirls with glee,
My unseen pals are there with me.

The rug lets out a tiny sigh,
Every footstep, a gentle high,
Together we weave, day by day,
In this quiet, we find our play.

The Power of Presence

In the fridge, a pickle grins,
Cheering up my veggie sins,
As I munch, it whispers, 'Hey,
You know it's fun to be this way!'

The cat rolls over, all aloof,
But in its purr, there's hidden truth,
A fuzzy smile in every pause,
This is the life with no set laws.

A chair with arms like an embrace,
Softly supports my busy race,
With snacks and laughs, it knows my tale,
In its comfort, I cannot fail.

Every silence fills with lore,
A little magic I adore,
For in presence, even quite,
Is a friendship shining bright.

Invisible Threads

In the corner, socks conspire,
One's a thief, the other's a liar.
Tangled, twisted, in the wash,
Dancing around like a silly nosh.

They giggle behind a folded T-shirt,
Caught in a spin, they frolic and flirt.
Hiding away from the world so bright,
Stitching up laughter each laundry night.

Silently plotting their great escape,
While the jeans demand a change of shape.
Sneaky sneakers slip off the rack,
Whispering jokes during the snack attack.

But come the dawn, they form a line,
Look sharp, folks, it's laundry time!
Rolling on wheels, their secret dare,
Invisible threads weave through the air.

Muted Moments

In a teacup, the spoons have a chat,
While the sugar cubes dress like a brat.
Coffee slurps, while the cream just sighs,
Rolling its eyes, oh what a surprise!

Saucers spin tales of faraway lands,
Whisking away with invisible hands.
They dream of trips in a cozy pot,
Hiding the secrets that they forgot.

The kettle erupts with a chuckle and beep,
It's time for the brew, no time for sleep!
Chatter rings out as they toast and gleam,
In muted moments, they share a dream.

Shy Companions

Under the bed where dust bunnies play,
A sock goes missing, it's gone astray.
The other pair hides in a drawer,
Tiptoeing softly, they want to explore.

Whispering secrets, out of plain sight,
They plan their escape on a starry night.
A cap and a shoe join the escapade,
Sipping on moonlight, laughing, charade.

Tables are set for a silly feast,
The napkins party with a comedy beast.
Shy companions under the pale moonlight,
Share laughter and secrets, just out of sight.

Distant Heartbeats

In the attic, a clock ticks loud,
While an old chair creaks, feeling proud.
Dust motes dance in the beams of sun,
They chuckle along, just having fun.

An umbrella waits, dreaming of rain,
While a lonely hat collects some disdain.
Cousin's sweater winks and says, 'Hey!'
Thinking of days when they'd leap and play.

In a closet, a shy shoe says, 'No!'
When the other calls out, 'Come on, let's go!'
Distant heartbeats make a ruckus so sweet,
As they plot their adventure, can't take a seat.

Silent Affinities

Two socks sit in a drawer,
In a world with no noise.
They share tales of the floor,
In their mismatched poise.

A cat naps with a shrug,
On a pile of old clothes.
Dreams of catching a bug,
While the dust softly glows.

A teapot whispers with pride,
Though no one's made tea.
Her steamy tales, they glide,
Only for birds to see.

A pair of shoes in line,
With laces all yanked tight.
They await the next sign,
For a wild, fun-filled night.

Quiet Kindred

Two chairs creak in delight,
As friends who rarely speak.
They sway in the soft light,
Sipping silence each week.

A table wobbles sly,
Planning pranks on the cat.
It giggles deep inside,
While the dog's just flat.

A clock watches the game,
But ticks in total hush.
Feeling rather quite lame,
When there's no one to rush.

An empty swing set swings,
With laughter from the past.
Echoing silly things,
That forever will last.

The Language of Stillness

A rock boasts of its age,
In the garden's green field.
It flips through each page,
Of history revealed.

A shoehorn tells the tale,
Of how it came to be.
To fit snugly without fail,
In perfect harmony.

A forgotten old mug,
Hides tales of morning brews.
Caffeine dreams, quite a snug,
In soft, ceramic hues.

A broom sweeps without fuss,
As it waltzes along.
In the quiet of us,
It hums a gentle song.

Unheard Melodies

A pillow snores at night,
Beneath a head full of dreams.
It knows the whispered plight,
Of secrets and soft schemes.

A curtain flirts with the breeze,
As it dances with grace.
No one sees its expertise,
In the quiet headspace.

A glove hides in the dark,
In a drawer full of plight.
It longs for a small spark,
To pair up and take flight.

A shadow waits in glee,
For an unsuspecting friend.
It chuckles silently,
As the day starts to end.

Silent Partnerships

In a room with just the cat,
Whiskers twitch, looking fat.
He plots to steal my lunch,
A daring little munch.

With socks that vanish, oh so sly,
They hide and seek, but never die.
They make a mess, these little things,
Yet bring me joy, their laughter sings.

Invisible pals on my late-night snack,
A ghostly sound, the pantry's crack.
I talk to walls; they seem to grin,
My humorous chaos, where to begin?

So here's to those in silent cheer,
With playful pranks, they disappear.
Their quiet ways, a subtle tease,
In goofy moments, I'm at ease.

Embracing the Unsaid

The couch holds tales that never squeak,
Pillows gossip, oh so meek.
Fluffy friends, they nod in glee,
As secrets shared, just them and me.

In the fridge sits a steadfast jar,
Pickles as partners, near and far.
Though dressed in brine, they always cheer,
Tasting laughter, year by year.

I stroll with shadows, think they're sly,
Playing tricks as they pass by.
A smile exchanged, a quiet grin,
In this wacky game, we all win.

The TV remote, a loyal mate,
Hides from me at the strangest rate.
Yet when I find it, we dance about,
In this silent waltz, there's never doubt.

Hidden Presences

Under the bed, dust bunnies wait,
Yearning for dinner off my plate.
With tiny whispers, they conspire,
Plotting mischief, fueling desire.

My forgotten chair tells tales of woe,
Of books once read and coffee's flow.
It creaks and squeaks, a buddy true,
In moments bland, it makes me woo.

The clock ticks softly, sings to me,
Racing time, in playful glee.
One beat off, it lags behind,
Keeping secrets, never unkind.

So raise a toast to things unseen,
Their funny antics, a subtle sheen.
In every corner, laughter grows,
These hidden pals, everyone knows.

Serene Confidants

The plant in the corner, leafy green,
Whispers wisdom from the unseen.
Its photosynthesis, a perfect ploy,
Foliage sways, a silent joy.

The dog outside, a digging expert,
Unveils treasures, what a concert!
He barks at squirrels, as if to say,
'Life's a game, let's play all day!'

A chair with a squeak, oh so sly,
Keeps me company when I sigh.
Each creak sends laughter up the hall,
My furniture friends, they're having a ball!

So here we are, in quiet cheer,
With giggles hiding, ever near.
In a world where silence sings,
These serene pals bring all the flings.

Fleeting Whispers

In shadows they wiggle and squirm,
Like socks on a floor, they all yearn.
A laugh in the stillness, a silly sound,
Invisible ribbons tie friendship around.

They play hide and seek with the night,
Sneaking a peek, oh what a sight!
Like echoes of giggles in lightly dim light,
These silent chums make everything bright.

In corners they gather to share what they think,
A toss of emotions, a nod, and a wink.
A wink is worth plenty, well, at least two,
Together they ponder the sights old and new.

Floating like dust in the beam of the sun,
The whispers of laughter is never quite done.
They nudge and they poke with a gentler grace,
With humor entwined, they lighten the space.

Unvoiced Connections

In the corner, they chuckle and cheer,
A band of shadows, inconspicuous here.
No one will notice their playful debate,
Yet together, they still contemplate fate.

Their quirks are absorbed in bright summer air,
Like an awkward dance with invisible flair.
Footsteps unheard, yet causing a stir,
Bantering softly, but never demur.

They pull at your sleeve with giggles unsaid,
A chorus of chuckles, with laughter widespread.
Like old pals at a gathering, scattered yet near,
In their quietness, nothing they fear.

A tickle in silence, a jab through the night,
Their humor wraps softly, like a warm, fuzzy light.
Giggling alone, yet bound as a clique,
In the hush of the moment, they softly speak.

Still Companionship

In the stillness, they quietly grin,
Like leaves in the breeze, they enjoy the spin.
Dancing through shadows, their whispers ignite,
Echoing laughter, a delightful sight.

Among the mundane, they silently jest,
No need for chatter, they're simply the best.
Like bubbles in soda, they pop with a laugh,
Turning the ordinary to a joyful path.

In corners and creases, they find their way,
Mischief afoot, they play it away.
Without a sound, they spark of delight,
A tapestry woven of sheer moonlight.

They shimmy and sway, unbidden, unseen,
Chasing their shadows in joyous routine.
While everyone's busy, they shimmer and wink,
With each little giggle, the soul starts to think.

Gentle Presence

Invisible buddies with a sense of fun,
They roll like thunder without a gun.
Poking at humor in soft, secret ways,
Brightening dull and forgettable days.

They whisper and laugh at the edges of sight,
A merry parade in the briskness of night.
As mouths stay mum, eyes twinkle and spark,
Creating a dance in the chilly, dark park.

Each shuffle and giggle, a secretive glee,
Bound by the humor, just them and the spree.
Like figures in comic strips, vivid and light,
They weave their delight in delightfully bright.

With each subtle nudge, they conjure a cheer,
Their quiet rejoicing draws everyone near.
In jest and in jibe, they fly on their quest,
The most playful presence, a heartfelt jest.

Tranquil Ties

In the corner, a sock awaits,
Whispers of warmth, it celebrates.
A pillow's sigh, so soft and round,
Bouncing thoughts without a sound.

Cuddly toys with watchful eyes,
Plotting adventures under the skies.
The couch rolls its eyes, holds its breath,
As snacks tiptoe past, defying death.

The cat napping, with expert grace,
Chasing dreams in this cozy space.
While dust bunnies conspire, unseen,
In this home, it reigns serene.

A teacup laughs, it will not spill,
Sharing secrets, it loves the thrill.
As curtains sway, the light peeks in,
Who knew the quiet could be so grim?

Echoes of Affection

A spoon and fork in a drawer lie,
Arguing softly, oh my, oh my!
The fridge hums a comforting tune,
While laughter spills from the bright blue moon.

A rubber duck with an air of pride,
Floats in waters, untroubled, wide.
Each wave a giggle, bubbling bliss,
In their own world, sweet, cozy bliss.

The clock ticks gently, keeping time,
Counting moments, rhythm, and rhyme.
As socks spin tales on the washing line,
Bouncing laughter, oh, how they shine!

The dust settles lightly, with charm it finds,
As books share stories of dazzling minds.
In this embrace of soft delight,
Where whispers are plenty; the shadows ignite.

Soft Footfalls

Pitter-patter of tiny feet,
A mouse and a kitten, a grand retreat.
Sneaky snacks from the pantry drawer,
While our shadows dance on the floor.

Beneath the couch, a rogue shoe lies,
Holding secrets, away from prying eyes.
As echoes of laughter drift through the air,
A playful glint that leads us there.

A friendly broom with a sweeping grin,
Scattering crumbs and old within.
As chairs creak softly, tired from play,
They whisper tales of the day-to-day.

And lighthearted spirits float around,
With trusty companions that we've found.
In this quirky haven, giggles croon,
Where silence bursts forth like a wild balloon!

Timid Alliances

The rug hides the secrets we dare to tell,
As whispers mingle, casting a spell.
The wallflowers chuckle, dance out of sight,
Where the dust motes twirl in beams of light.

Tiny pencils with minds so grand,
Crafting doodles, a sketchy band.
While paper clips wrestle, a hilarious sight,
In tidy chaos, they find delight.

A lone mug proclaims, "I hold the best brew!"
While spoons play hopscotch, just me and you.
In this realm of silence and silly quips,
The joy of the stillness, it surely grips.

A friendship blooms, unspoken, yet bold,
In cozy corners, our stories unfold.
As curtains bow to the magic we find,
In the company of quirks, we're intertwined.

The Language of Silence

Whispers in the air, so light,
Where words would surely scare the night.
A nod, a wink, a playful grin,
In silence, we let mischief begin.

We share our jokes without a sound,
In quiet, laughter knows no bound.
A raised eyebrow, a tilted head,
In the hush, our humor is widespread.

With smirks and giggles, we conspire,
In stillness, our antics never tire.
While others chatter, we play our game,
The mute duo, but never the same.

In silence, we're loud, we're bold, we're bright,
With every glance, we delight in the night.
No need for noise, our bond is clear,
In quiet companionship, we cheer!

Soothe the Unsaid

Sitting snug without a word,
In comfort, our thoughts are stirred.
A look towards the frosted glass,
No need for chatter, just let it pass.

When teacups clink with no one near,
We giggle softly, it's crystal clear.
A shared secret beneath a frown,
In silence, we wear our silly crown.

Sometimes we dance with a subtle sway,
While the world around us fades away.
Our hearts converse in the playful hush,
In every pause, there's a gentle rush.

With just a smile, the room ignites,
In silent pacts, we scale new heights.
Words can wait, we've got our way,
In sweetest silence, we always play!

Shadows of Understanding

Beneath the stars, we share our space,
In shadows deep, we find our grace.
A gesture here, a finger's twirl,
In quiet nights, our stories unfurl.

The world may shout, but we just grin,
With muted hearts, our joy begins.
Each raised hand, a signal sent,
In laughter's silence, we find content.

When life's a puzzle, we just smirk,
With unspoken words, we do the work.
In every pause, a comic tale,
Our chuckles echo, like a light sail.

So here we stand, no need for sound,
In quietude, our laughs abound.
With every glance, we weave our fate,
In shadows soft, we simply relate.

Still Waters

In tranquil pools, we float along,
Without a word, we hum our song.
Each timid wave is just for fun,
In placid reign, we've already won.

A smile flits like a fish below,
In stillness, our laughter starts to flow.
Bubbles rise and burst like dreams,
In quiet waters, joy's not what it seems.

The ripples dance in the evening light,
With unvoiced secrets that feel just right.
We splash and play, no words to say,
In gentle waves, we won't delay.

Just two quiet souls in silky sighs,
Making magic without goodbyes.
From the surface, our smiles ignite,
In still waters, we find our flight.

Deep Truths

Amidst the echoes of silence divine,
We find our truths in the quiet line.
No grand speeches, no shouting loud,
In whispers soft, we wear our shroud.

A simple glance, a knowing grin,
In subtlety, we let life begin.
With every pause, we strip away,
To uncover humor where silence plays.

We share the depths of all we know,
In the calmest moments, laughter grows.
Each nod a pact, each smile a cue,
In the stillness, our joy shines through.

So let the world around us blare,
In our quiet corner, we're quite the pair.
With giggles tucked in every deed,
In silent smiles, we plant the seed.

Heartfelt Absences

In the chair sits a cat, so relaxed,
Yet the house feels empty, and quite taxed.
With a flick of her tail, she dreams of the sun,
But I swear there's a ghost — oh, this house is fun!

A sock on the floor is my only mate,
It listens to secrets, no need for debate.
While I sip my tea, it doesn't judge me,
Just patiently waits for our next cup of glee.

The fridge hums a tune, my late-night friend,
Together we dance as we munch to no end.
I trip on a broom that has feelings and cares,
Guess that's why I talk to inanimate pairs!

The books on the shelf, they giggle and sigh,
Each turn of a page brings a silent reply.
With each little whisper, they keep me in stitches,
Life's surprises are small, but I love all my glitches.

The Stillness Between

In the middle of chaos, there's a broom that can dance,
With a handle so long, it gives dust a chance.
My old trusty chair, creaky and wise,
Shares tales of the past, and I just roll my eyes.

Two plants on the sill have the juiciest gossip,
They chatter away while they sip on a drop.
I tell them my secrets, they keep them just right,
Only I know they don't talk back at night!

The fridge takes a breath, a cool serenade,
While leftovers plot an escape from the trade.
The clock on the wall seems to chuckle a beat,
Tick-tock goes the banter — oh, life is a treat!

A cushion that cushions my ponderous thoughts,
Winks every time I forget about knots.
Though silence can seem like a void in the day,
With friends like these, who needs chatter anyway?

Ghostly Companionship

There's a ghost in the attic, or so I've been told,
I bet he just wants a few stories retold.
He rattles in laughter, but mostly he sighs,
Just eager to hear how the world never dies.

The vacuum and I have a love-hate affair,
He grumbles and whirs, yet we make quite the pair.
While I dodge his suction, he rolls with a glee,
Planning all sorts of tricks, just to annoy me!

Potted plants lean in, whispering tales,
Of shadows at dusk and of brisk autumn gales.
I can't help but chuckle, we're quite the odd lot,
In this funny old house, we tie each other's knots.

The cobwebs take credit for stories of old,
Each thread spun with care, are like secrets retold.
In silence, we're loud, and in idleness, brave,
Glimpsing the beauty where echoes misbehave.

Harmony in Hushed Tones

The teacup's a diva, it sings when it clinks,
While under the table, a sandwich winks.
My slippers have laughter, as soft as a sigh,
Making each step feel like clouds passing by.

The walls hold their breath when I start to hum,
Feeling the rhythm, oh, what have I done?
The curtains sway gently, tapping their toes,
Joining in merriment — who knew this could grow?

The clock joins the choir, with a tick and a tock,
Pacing the beat like a quirky old rock.
With every soft echo and little parade,
It's silent pandemonium — magic we made!

So here in the stillness, with laughter so bright,
I lose track of time in this whimsical light.
For life can be fun, in spaces unseen,
Where shadows are playful, and we dance in between!

Ghosts of Friendship

In shadows they linger, a chuckle or two,
Invisible pals, with a wacky view.
They whisper sly jokes, in the dead of the night,
Yet leave me alone when it's time for a fright.

With flickers of laughter, they dance on the wall,
Haunting my laughter, they're having a ball.
Their midnight performances, ghostly delight,
Leave me in stitches, till dawn's early light.

Guardian of Secrets

A bubble of laughter, a wink and a grin,
They cradle my secrets, where to begin?
In the cloak of the quiet, they giggle and sway,
Protecting my whispers in their own sly way.

Like ninjas of silence, they scamper around,
Eavesdropping softly, without making a sound.
They guard my confessions, with a cheeky jest,
In the realm of hilarity, they're truly the best.

The Weight of Quietude

In the stillness they settle, a plump pillow cloud,
Making silence lighter, not too serious or loud.
They lounge in my thoughts, with a wink and a sigh,
As if cracking jokes, while the world passes by.

With giggles unspoken and snickers unheard,
They play on my heartstrings, a soft, funny chord.
In moments of peace, they spark a bright cheer,
Turning my frown into a chuckle, my dear!

Soft Footfalls

Pitter-patter laughter, they tiptoe with glee,
Sneaking up gently, just to tease me.
Their soft, silent steps, like a lighthearted rhyme,
Keep my spirits soaring, every tick of the time.

Between the tick-tock, they play hide and seek,
With silent snorts, every nudge's unique.
In the absence of noise, they frolic and flinch,
Making each quiet wink, a whimsical pinch.

Still Waters Run Deep

In the pond, a frog croaks loud,
Reminding me he's quite the proud.
He jumps and splashes, what a scene,
I laugh at him, the pond's big queen.

A turtle sunbathes with grace so slow,
He thinks he's fast, he simply won't go.
With a wink and a nod, the fish just swim,
While the lily pads giggle at every whim.

The dragonflies dance, a silly ballet,
They buzz by my ear as if to say,
"We're having a party, come join the fun,
Just watch for the splash—it's what we've done!"

Amongst the stillness, chaos does reign,
Nature's antics, the best in the game.
With laughter I watch the show unfold,
In quiet waters, excitement untold.

Echoes of the Unseen

In the attic, the shadows play,
A mouse scurries, chasing a stray.
It squeaks a tune, oh so out of tune,
As my cat pounces, like a cartoon.

Beneath the floor, the creaks and groans,
Are ghosts maybe, or just old bones?
They whisper tales, both silly and bold,
Of socks gone missing, and treasures untold.

Outside the window, a squirrel does prance,
With nuts in his cheeks, he's ready to dance.
He leaps and he bounds, a zany routine,
His antics are fit for a stand-up scene.

In every corner, a giggle will rise,
With whispers and squeaks, a joyful surprise.
In the silence, a ruckus erupts,
In unseen echoes, the laughter erupts.

Subdued Comforts

On the couch, a blanket fights,
With the dog stealing it through the nights.
Pillows are strewn, a fortress built,
In the cozy mess, there's naught but guilt.

The cat's on the shelf, plotting her heist,
With eyes like jewels, she's not very nice.
A tumble, a thud, her mission's in flight,
As I sip my tea, she stirs up the night.

A shadow, a flicker, what could it be?
The toast pops up, it's just my cup of tea!
But the kettle whistles, a high-pitched scream,
It's the only way to shatter the dream.

Among the cushions, laughter runs deep,
Socks in the fridge, it's time for some sleep.
In this thoughtful chaos, comfort's the key,
In subdued shenanigans, joy is in spree.

Whispers in the Shadows

A raccoon picks through the midnight trash,
With eyes aglow, he makes quite the splash.
He's got some moves, a nimble little thief,
In moonlight's glow, he's lost in belief.

The owl hoots low, a wise old sage,
While the bats swoop down, unwritten page.
What tales do they tell in the chilly night?
I suspect they've partied; oh, what a sight!

In the garden, the gnomes whisper jokes,
About curious cats and peculiar folks.
They tip their hats and chuckle with glee,
As a hedgehog rolls by, feeling carefree.

The stars are twinkling, secrets galore,
While fireflies flicker, asking for more.
In shadows undisturbed, laughter resounds,
With whispers of joy in the night, it abounds.

Silent Shadows

In corners they linger, oh what a sight,
With fluttering faces, all lost in the light.
They cheerfully creep, avoiding the fuss,
Whispering tales, like they're all on the bus.

They dance on the wall, just out of the breeze,
Mimicking antics like squirrels in trees.
A twirl and a shimmy without making sound,
In this silent ballet, pure joy can be found.

They're masters of stealth, such sneaky old friends,
With jokes that they share, the laughter transcends.
In games of charades, they can't lose the match,
Those quirky companions, with charm they'll dispatch.

So if you should see them, give them a grin,
For silly old shadows, oh where to begin?
In the heart of the hush, they know how to play,
Join in their fun, let your worries give way.

Whispering Winds

They tickle the trees, where the branches get jiggy,
With secrets and giggles, so light, yet so wiggy.
A breeze swirls around, saying, 'Look at that guy!',
Gossiping softly, as they scatter and fly.

They poke at your hair with a playful embrace,
Chatting and chortling, they never leave space.
Just when you think they're a serious mess,
They're whispering jokes and causing a guess.

As if holding court in a carnival tent,
They caper and prance, in a cyclone they're sent.
With ticklish confessions they roam every street,
Invisible jesters that can't be beat.

So dance with the zephyrs, let laughter abound,
For in every gust, there's hilarity found.
The world gets a chuckle, spun round in delight,
In breezy companionship, spirits take flight.

Unseen Allies

In every small room, they hide with such care,
With quirks that keep bubbling, like thoughts in the air.
They play peek-a-boo from the shelf to the chair,
These friends made of nonsense, beyond compare.

They clash with your thoughts, like a riddle or joke,
With puns on their lips, they uplift and provoke.
Turning mundane moments into wild delight,
With antics they know will keep spirits in flight.

Their laughter unseen, yet it echoes around,
In the folds of the silence, their joy can be found.
They beam with a grin, painted bright like the sun,
In tricky disguise, they're still the most fun.

So when you feel low, or the day's turning gray,
Just look for those allies that brighten the way.
Behind every chuckle, there's magic, it's true,
Let unseen allies bring laughter to you.

The Stillness Between Us

In the pause of our chats, a giggle will bloom,
In that quiet between us, no hint of a gloom.
A knowing glance shared, no words need to speak,
With joy in each silence, our laughter's unique.

Sips of our drinks, we clink with delight,
In moments of stillness, the fun feels just right.
A smirk or a grin, can light up the air,
With jokes piled high, oh, the ease that we share.

We play at the edges of quiet and loud,
With humor that's formed in a giggling crowd.
Every glance a surprise, like a magic trick done,
In the stillness, we ponder, and burst into fun.

So cherish this bond, where the quiet can roar,
In shared, silent laughter, we're always wanting more.
For amidst the calm moments that dance all around,
The joy of this stillness is truly profound.

Tranquil Togetherness

In a cozy nook, they sit and chat,
Two silent friends, just like a cat.
Whispers of laughter, a giggle or two,
Sharing their secrets without much ado.

Tea cups clink softly, no words to be found,
But the joy in the air, oh, it knows no bound.
They trade goofy glances, smirks on their face,
In a world full of chatter, they've found their own space.

Lurking in shadows, a dance of the shy,
With a wave of a hand, they say their goodbye.
Though silence may linger, it's bold as a quip,
In their fortress of fun, they happily trip.

Together they beam, without a grand show,
The quiet's electric, like a silent disco.
With no need for noise, just a gut-wrenching laugh,
Two silly souls writing their own epitaph.

Shy Souls in Harmony

Two awkward ducks on a pond so still,
They quack out for comfort, but never for thrill.
Their laughter is muffled, like a soft pillow,
Chasing away sorrows, making hearts glow.

Whispers like snowflakes, they tumble to land,
Painting their joy with a delicate hand.
While others are loud, they giggle in fun,
Sailing on silence, oh, what could be done?

With nods that are clumsy and smiles full of joy,
They find all the odd things that childhood can toy.
Like two hidden treasures, they twinkle and sing,
A concert of chuckles, the joy they can bring.

In a world that's bustling, they take a slow stroll,
Two bashful souls sharing one hilarious goal.
Their bond's made of sparkles that shimmer and sway,
In a universe quiet, they conquer the day!

Invisible Connections

Floating like whispers, two giggles collide,
In the wild of the quiet, they take quite the ride.
No need for a stage, nor grand puppet show,
Just subtle connections that chuckle and glow.

Like cats in a box, they fit just right,
A world full of chatter, but they shun the blight.
Trading their nudges, a quick glance, a grin,
The joy in their eyes, where the laughter begins.

Invisible threads, they weave with delight,
Dancing through moments, in silence polite.
The stories unspoken, but oh, how they shine,
Making every pause feel just too divine.

So here's to the pair, who need not a sound,
In their own little bubble, they joyously bound.
Catching the giggles in soft cloudy skies,
Through whispers and chuckles, love never denies.

Petals on a Still Lake

Petals drifting softly, beneath the pale moon,
Two friends float on silence, humming a tune.
With each little ripple, a chuckle is borne,
In the midst of the calm, bright laughter is worn.

Like flowers in bloom, devoid of loud fuss,
They share their quirks quietly, just the two of us.
In the dance of the ducks, they find their own beat,
In the rhythm of silence, their lives feel complete.

Oh, the joy of the tender, unspoken delight,
With glances and grins in the hush of the night.
No need for a crowd or a raucous loud cheer,
In the garden of giggles, they make it all clear.

So here's to the moments when words are not found,
Their laughter in silence is beautifully sound.
Like petals on water, they gracefully sway,
Creating their melody in the calm of the day.

Muted Emotions

In a room where whispers dwell,
A couch lingers, its stories to tell.
It's seen the joy, the tears—oh dear!
Yet all it does is silently cheer.

A sock peeks out from under the chair,
It listens closely without a care.
Its mismatched color brings giggles in jam,
Much funnier than a live sitcom fam!

The cat napping soundly, a heavy snore,
While dreaming of things that it can't explore.
A feathered friend on the wall sits tight,
Judging the cat's very ungraceful flight.

So here's to the objects in slumber and sigh,
With laughter hidden, a twinkle in their eye.
They hold the memories of laughter and glee,
And the best part is—none charge a fee!

Reflections in Tranquility

A teacup giggles in a cupboard high,
Holding secrets like a spy on the sly.
With each sip that you take, it sighs loud,
Wishing to spill tales and join the crowd.

A potted plant gives advice through leaves,
Each green one grumbles, a sage who believes.
It nudges its friends, the dust bunnies low,
'At least we're not picking up the show!'

A book on the shelf lays open and bare,
With words too shy to jump in the air.
It tries to charm readers with a wink,
But covers its face when they start to think!

So in this quiet, a riot prevails,
As laughter flutters on soft, gentle sails.
Through unspoken jokes and shared delight,
The stillness is filled with humor so bright!

Hidden Harmonies

In a chest filled with trinkets of old,
A funky keychain has stories untold.
It jangles and laughs with every small shake,
'Remember that time? Oh, for goodness' sake!'

Beneath the rug, a dust mote brigade,
They dance and they twirl in an endless parade.
A sneeze sends them flying, oh what a sight!
They giggle and scatter, they're quite a delight!

The clock ticks away, in its rhythm it grins,
Counting the moments where mischief begins.
With each tick it whispers sly little jokes,
While causing a ruckus with old-fashioned pokes.

So let's tap our toes on this hidden beat,
Where laughter and hush in a shuffle compete.
For in every shadow, a riddle's tucked in,
With harmonies sweet, let the fun times begin!

Veiled Conversations

A curtain sways, holding voices so tight,
It giggles behind while dimming the light.
Holding its breath with a swish and a swoosh,
It mimics the waves of a nearby bush.

Two spoons in a drawer, they trade little jests,
'Here's to the days we've survived all the tests!'
They clink as they greet, a metallic cheer,
With stories of soup and sweet loving cheer.

The fridge hums a tune, its melody bright,
While leftovers croon under the soft night light.
They whisper their secrets in plastic-wrapped dreams,
As flavors collide in uncanny regimes.

So in every corner, a giggle remains,
In silence and stillness, where humor complains.
Through veils of soft whispers and silly old tricks,
Life holds sweet moments—no need for the scripts!

Unexpressed Harmony

In a room filled with chatter, silence plays,
Invisible musicians in calm ballet.
Hands wave like wildflowers, but lips stay tight,
Guess the tune, oh what a sight!

Tickles of laughter hide behind shy grins,
Making round sounds like unmarked pins.
A nod, a smile, a wink in the air,
Creating a symphony without a care.

Chairs squeak in rhythm, a proper dance,
Footsteps soft as whispers, leading a chance.
In the overlap of silence and jest,
Who knew quiet moments could be the best?

Oh, the unspoken jokes they weave and twine,
In every glance, a hidden punchline.
Who needs words when we've got this fun?
A congress of mimes and laughter's undone!

Moments of Stillness

In a cafe where chatter buzzes like bees,
Two souls sip coffee, just enjoying the tease.
Their eyes do the talking, without any sound,
In moments of stillness, so profound.

The clink of the cup offers a gentle cheer,
While laughter echoes from corners, it's clear.
A pause in the chaos, a look and a grin,
Who needs a script when you're on the same whim?

Time ticks away, lost in playful thoughts,
Every sip shared, a bottle of shots.
With a slurp and a sigh, they give each other fits,
In this quiet café, they revel in fits.

So let the world buzz and the people all rush,
In their moments of stillness, they'll forever shush.
For friendship's a secret, soft as a song,
Nestled in silence, where they both belong.

The Beauty of Bated Breath

In waiting so quiet, we hold our delight,
Eyes wide and expectant, a comical sight.
When minutes go by, like molasses in dreams,
Breath caught in laughter, or so it seems.

The clock ticks like a drummer, keeping its beat,
A party of thoughts beneath the discreet.
We wait for the punchline, hands up like a band,
With wide eyes and giggles, we're ready to stand!

The build-up's a riddle, oh what a jest,
Collecting our breath for the very best quest.
In the pauses between, we stumble and roam,
Creating our laughter, the funniest home.

A deep breath in, and a chuckle out loud,
As the moment breaks forth, we're both quite proud.
For laughter will find us, in breath, it will bloom,
In this beauty of waiting, we lock in the room.

In the Company of Shadows

In corners they linger, shadows that play,
With antics and mischief, come what may.
While others may chatter, they whisper in spree,
In the company of shadows, we giggle with glee.

Poking and prodding, they tease and they taunt,
Being quiet's an art, oh how it can haunt!
Instead of the spotlight, they bask in the gloom,
Where shadows take form, and humor finds room.

Lurking in sunlight, they dance out of place,
Returning to ink, like a scribbled embrace.
With just a quick flick, they jump, dive, and spin,
Creating a comedy only we get to win.

So here in the dusk, where their laughter runs wild,
Shadows become friends, like the heart of a child.
In the company of stillness, absurd and askew,
Together we laugh, with nothing to do!

Found in the Stillness.

In the room, a sock just grins,
It's had its fill of silent spins.
A chair that rocks, a cat that snores,
They laugh at life without much roars.

The fridge hums tunes of midnight snacks,
While the calendar shades in all my lacks.
The dust bunnies dance with glee,
As they plan a party just for me.

A lonely spoon sits on the shelf,
It dreams of being used, not just itself.
With every clang and clatter, who knew?
The forks and knives feel lonely too!

In the stillness, time takes a bait,
And every little tick seems like a date.
With laughter wrapped in silence thick,
Even solitude can pull a trick.

Silent Shadows

Under the table, shadows play,
They make all the old things sway.
A playful ghost with a friendly grin,
Makes the night feel like a win.

The lightbulb flickers — what a show!
Rolling laughter from the window,
The curtains dance with every breeze,
They whisper jokes that bring us ease.

A shadow hops, not making sound,
In its world, silliness is abound.
With a wink and a nod, they clink their cups,
And toast to life with bubbly ups!

Yet, when the moon shines bright and wide,
They form a queue to take a ride.
Silly shapes come into view,
As shadows laugh and bid adieu.

Whispering Winds

The wind slips past with jokes to share,
Teasing leaves without a care.
Twisting branches in a dance,
While clouds overhead dream of romance.

A gusty breeze carries a giggle,
As butterflies perform their wiggle.
They flit about on unseen strings,
While the daisies chuckle at silly things.

With every puff, the tale unfolds,
Of secret whispers the cosmos holds.
Trees sway softly in giddy delight,
Their laughter echoed deep in the night.

And as the sun begins to set,
The winds hum softly, no regret.
With playful sighs, they swirl and spin,
In the air, the fun begins again.

Subtle Echoes

In empty halls, the echoes ring,
A voice that laughs, a happy thing.
Whispers bounce from wall to wall,
Bringing joy to the quiet hall.

The floorboards creak with tales untold,
Every sound seems a bit too bold.
A chipmunk giggles, runs on by,
While echoes sing a playful cry.

A gentle thud, a sneaky slide,
And the echoes seem to like the ride.
They weave a story, soft yet loud,
Bringing little giggles from the crowd.

In this stillness, fun's afoot,
With every sound, the joy is put.
Subtle echoes, a charming game,
In the quiet, never the same.

Echoes of Solitude

In corners dark, the shadows sway,
Whispering jokes from yesterday.
A pair of socks that lost their mate,
In laughter's grip, they contemplate.

The dust bunnies huddle, talking cheer,
Sharing tales from far and near.
Curled up socks find a cozy nook,
While the cat investigates the book.

A lonely chair begins to chuckle,
As cozy blankets softly snuggle.
The goldfish rolls its little eye,
Witnessing the world swim by.

With every creak, a joke is spun,
In silent moments, enter fun.
The echoes of silence tickle the air,
Our unseen friends lounge everywhere.

Gentle Presence

In sunlight's gleam, the pillows grin,
As lazy cats plot ways to win.
A mug half full, a spoon in tow,
Stirs up laughter from last night's show.

The clock chimes softly, can't take its time,
Winks at the teapot, oh, what a crime!
They clink and clank, a merry band,
Sipping secrets brewed so grand.

A missing shoe starts a running spree,
Telling tales that just can't be.
With every shuffle, giggles grow,
As mates of mischief steal the show.

In corners where the light is dim,
The laughter spreads, it does not skim.
With lighthearted sighs, a sense of glee,
In quiet spots, fun runs free.

Unvoiced Conversations

A plant in a pot, with leaves so bright,
Whispers softly at the moon's light.
While dust motes dance in perfect time,
Companions of silence—oh, how they chime!

The couch sits proud, though springs may squeak,
In cushy corners, it's laughter we seek.
An old throw pillow tells tales of yore,
As it dreams of glory, what's behind the door?

A forgotten sandwich, well, that's the joke,
It's sprouting stories, now that it's woke.
The fridge hums low with secrets to share,
In unvoiced chuckles, it fills the air.

In each silent heartbeat, hilarity weights,
A symphony of whispers that never waits.
In the hush, we find joy intertwined,
With unspoken laughter, oh so refined.

Hushed Moments

The curtains sway, like they've got the moves,
As sunlight giggles, it surely proves.
The toaster pops, a crispy surprise,
And even the burnt bread can't hide its guise.

In soft, gentle airs, a cat's meow sings,
Of teasing the mouse and other small things.
A dust moted whisper, on a breeze it floats,
Bringing laughter in silent anecdotes.

A forgotten hat, on a shelf it glows,
It wears its legacy, nobody knows.
With every tick from the old grandfather clock,
Time holds punchlines, tickled to shock.

In every hush, a quirky tune plays,
Filling the quiet in funny ways.
So here's to moments, serene yet bright,
Where laughter hides in the softest light.

www.ingramcontent.com/pod-product-compliance
Lightning Source LLC
Chambersburg PA
CBHW072218070526
44585CB00015B/1390